The Cost of Living

The
New Works
Of
merrit malloy

iUniverse LLC
Bloomington

iUniverse books may be ordered through booksellers or by contacting:

iUniverse
1663 Liberty Drive
Bloomington, IN 47403
www.iuniverse.com
1-800-Authors (1-800-288-4677)

Because of the dynamic nature of the Internet, any web addresses or links contained in this book may have changed since publication and may no longer be valid. The views expressed in this work are solely those of the author and do not necessarily reflect the views of the publisher, and the publisher hereby disclaims any responsibility for them.

Any people depicted in stock imagery provided by Thinkstock are models, and such images are being used for illustrative purposes only.

Certain stock imagery © Thinkstock.

ISBN: 978-1-4759-8105-6 (sc)
ISBN: 978-1-4759-8106-3 (e)

Printed in the United States of America

iUniverse rev. date: 7/29/2013

A Note From the Author

The title of this book is somewhat deceiving.
These pages are not about
THE COST OF LIVING,
they are really about
THE COST OF NOT LIVING.

According to the same laws
that hold us down,
We can rise up
...We can take noise and turn it
into a song

As William Butler Yeats so wisely
said "It is not our task as writers to
make poetry but to make more poets."

It has take me years on <u>NOT</u> writing
to write this page.

This book is for Jack Riley,
who is the love of my life.

And..

These pages are dedicated to whatever moves us
towards each other which returns us
(finally) to ourselves

Table of Contents

The Cost of Living

For a long time I've been laying track out ahead of this page
I am learning trust by going on beyond the place
where a thousand voices have told me to turn back
I am attempting to do what they say cannot be done
I am crossing the barriers of other men's things and
entering my own

This is that sacred place that one cannot get to
except by bringing it forth This is where
one utterly risks one's life in order to restore it
Born of our own violation This might (and has)
been named Dominion
Call it anything you like
it's wholly yours

The cost of living
and I mean the cost or REALLY living
of BEING alive appears (finally) to be in the act of bringing forth
out of nothing but ourselves
In the actions that we take as we continue to go on beyond the place
where the road ends andto do thc things that can't be done
to stand on your own words as a paratrooper stands on air
risking all is how we get it all

This is the abyss where we must all jump
nothing to hold us yet we are not dropped we are lifted
by the fall (carried maybe) these are the times
when we must go forward and when there doesn't appear to be a way
except to surrender everything

continued

And only when you do does the road return
only then do you know for sure that the thousand voices
who tried to stop you
were stopped themselves

You don't have to do this, of course
you have free will..you can just simply go on living
But if you want to REALLY BE ALIVE
you must dare to live your life as if your life depended on it
because in every way that matters
you're the only one who can

The cost of living is the action you take
in the face of not really BEING alive
To be appropriate to life, we must meet it squarely at every turn
we are equal to life according to our willingness to participate with it
to accept it as it is as it accepts us
to express it as eloquently as it has expressed us
this (finally) is the cost of being truly alive.

I say 'cost' limited by the language that does not yet include the simplicity
of this exchange
It is not actually a cost to be paid...More it is measured as completion
it is simply where one thing meets another so perfectly that each
completes the other
To HAVE life, we must BE life
If there is a cost so to speak
it is to match it not to pay
...to pay is how we miss the point

The Loyals

"I need you" says I want something
"I love you" says I accept you

Love doesn't ask for love, it is love
Love is an answer, not a question

I'd like you to care about me
but I won't stop loving you
if you don't

Love doesn't ask; it allows

The loyals aren't the ones who stay
when it gets rough
or even the ones that stay the longest

The loyals are the ones
who are already
there

The Partnership

As the actor knows
We deal in illusion

The camera's job is to trick us into
seeing

And the actor takes our place
in the photograph

It's the craftsman
who trusts in mystery
who tricks himself
into not knowing

If a performance touches you,
you did
half

Ying & Yang

If you marry a guy
You don't love;
…You'll probably
End up loving a guy
You can't marry

The Way He Wears His Hat

What can I say that describes him?
He's a man who eats cookies in bed
and makes birthday cards, by hand
...He still uses a blade shaver, tooth powder and
he doesn't own a tux, and in
most of the photographs,
he's smiling

There is a way he is with children
that meets them squarely and
joins them in <u>their own</u>
excitement...By being their <u>partner</u>,
he teaches them luck

Cole Porter was right, people come and go
but something stays - "the way they wear their hats,
the way they hold their forks"
...There is no blindness that takes away
what we've seen with love

I can try to tell you about him in words
but it's in how <u>I feel</u>
that actually describes
him

How we are measured

You get what you give. That's the law.
I didn't make that up.

It's okay to get what we want from somebody
but the real measure of ourselves
isn't in what we get from somebody else but
in what we have given them

Life

Life is not the opposite of death;
Life is the absence of it

Woman's Work

If you don't watch out
Men will start to write you letters about how they feel
…This is worse than getting flowers

And when they dare to tell you
that they are frightened this is where
you have to draw the line…Romance is women's work,
men have their own pornography

If you're not on guard
Men will have you caring about them this is much worse
than when they careabout you…This is even worse than
getting married

I'm telling you, we have to be really careful when men
start to open their hearts…We have no defense for this
We are supposed to be the ones that open
They're supposed to be the ones that come and go
…This is turning nature inside out…This is more terrible than
chocolate cake

If you don't watch out, men will start to admire you and make you big.
This is not their job; This is ours
They're supposed to be the ones who get hard;
we're supposed to be the ones that turn THEM to gold
…How dare they reverse romance and turn it into love
This is even worse than
getting a diamond

…This is giving one

Priorities

Just as people who are really together
continue to be with each other when they are apart,
people who are not really together can't
actually be with each other no matter how
much time they spend together.

So, after all, we are only as close as we feel.
And in turn,
just as far away.

Being in the same place at the same time
is not an issue of geography or even proximity
...Alliance with another human being
is an essential gesture

And we are with people according to WHO we are
in relation to them; not WHERE we are in relation
to them So

No amount of time spent together will join
those who are not really joined...

Being close is not about GETTING together
It's about BEING together

How Yes includes No

Where there is judgment
there is always agreement
Get this and you can
rise above the scales

The imperfection
and the perfection
are just opinion
until they make the circle
and are the
same

This is how comics
make us laugh out loud
at secret
things

The Muse

It has been many years since I have tempted the muse
There have been whole seasons of no corn
I have often been brought to my knees
"Please let me be your writer again?"
This was the prayer that always bent me down in shame

Earlier on this ride I had broken laws
I took the gifts given me and turned them into weapons
I twisted language from a tool into a stick and
I used words to hit people
I forgot that writing was a privilege…This was how
I was narrowed to a technician and came
to be forbidden at holy work
I used the words to serve myself and soon enough
my music turned to little stones

For many years, I told this story like it wasn't about me
Terrified of being seen, I turned at every light
I withdrew from every human hand and called it progress
Not being able to feel, I named my work a mystery
and raged ahead in neutral Turning,
Turning always turning

This was the journey without distance
that brought me in spirals
to my knees

-continued

"Please let me be a piano" I was asking to serve
and yet I could not give it
Not trusting I dug at every seed and ripped
apart the birthing grounds
until there was no more to come apart
Even at this there was (at least) a thousand days of silence

I was asking to be free yet I could not give it
This was how all I ever offered came
to nothing and how from nothing
All I could allow has come to this

I still do not understand what writes
these words nor what reads them
I only know that there is a third part of every
two who join a conduit, of some unknown sweetness
without which (or whom) I could not speak
to you at all This is the irony of letting go
that it returns

I'm not religious really, except to say that
I've come to trust the seed
I've noticed (as Einstein promised) that there is order here
so perfectly arranged that where there once was
nothing but little stones…There is corn again
and everywhere I turn
there is yellow all across the fields

What Doesn't Stop

Grief is not immeasurable
what's under rage is just
another asking
for love

Passion breaks us down and
forces us to look for beauty
in broken pieces of stone

At first the light can blind you
but love is a damn hard thing to kill
...no matter how we claw at it,
devotion does not come apart

I have ripped out my memory
looking for the seed
Love didn't start here yet
here's where it
continues...So

Grief is not immeasurable
It is just another part
of the asking

Fire

There was fire in us
A blind beauty
...It was innocent and
terrible

There was a fury in it
...a curious blaze of rage and faith,
competed for by glands and gods
and we encouraged it
blowing on the flames, moaning "yes, yes
oh yes"

From all this burning, it should be no wonder
to us what needs to be returned
nor onto whose shoulders
this rebuilding
will fall

Why are we always so surprised when we are asked
to give back what we have taken?

Communication

You either have a voice
or you don't
This is what I know
about singing
Listening is
the other half of this

You either know what I'm saying
or you don't
That's all I know about
communication

Hearing is another thing

Good Intentions (or what the road to hell is paved with)

I can't teach you anything
that I can't learn

I can only be here
as it happens

I had to think I was the only one
to be the
everyone
and

Without this there is
that

What holds us IS
the holding

There's the chicken
there's the egg
there's
everything

Getting What We Really Ask For

To give love to get love
is no more than giving attention
to get attention

If I'm good to you just because I want
you to be good to me
what I call love is
control

It's not the Attention
it's the Intention

We are not rewarded FOR our kindness
We are rewarded BY our
kindness

So if you really want to be cared for
try not to torture anyone into doing it

We get what we deserve
This is how we come to be afraid
And finally
This is how we come to be free

The Agreement

Hurt me, go ahead
At least it proves that
we are related to each other

Go on, I can take it just as hard
as you can give it
I'm just as strong as you are in
my weakness

We are in fear with each other
This is the cruel duet
This is why men kill their
brothers

So go on, let me have it
I can't lose because I can't win

As long as I wait for you to change
I get to be different
And being different is how I prove my fear of
being the same

Letting you hurt me is how I get you to
agree that I can hurt you

Logic

You say that something goes after many years
between a man and a woman I think that's true
But something stays, too
Something grows and something wanes something lifts
as things get heavier

And I wonder why we can't know this
until we have to
I wonder why we can't get more excited about
that which is given after years rather than mourn
that which we ourselves used up

Why can't we take what's left and restore it
replant it REinvent it...Hey
Better than a new mate
might be a new idea
More useful than divorce might be reunion
More perfect than silence may be the
spilling of the
beans

We shall finally have to do this with
our last mate, why not our first?
Because, after all

It isn't so much <u>who</u> we love that counts,
or even how many
...It's only that we
finally get it
right

Every Girl's Dream

If only
I could love myself
like I've loved
men

The Trap

He adored her, this is why she couldn't
stay with him

His asking was so big that she couldn't
use it up

He couldn't see who she was; only what she
Represented…This is how loyalty is corrupted and goes
wholly blind

His need to be the 'only' one
trapped him into wanting
the 'only' one

This is why he was a beggar in bed, it was a
Devotion…He was serving the outside God

And he cried because he was afraid of
what he wanted
and he (secretly) hated
what he loved

Progress

What a gigantic step it is
not to move

What We Resist We Can't Have

In order to run rapids,
you need to be wise enough to let the river take you
in its arms…To stiffen
would be a terrible mistake

…The river will just spit you out
or slam you like a thousand hands
into the deepest center lane where
your body will shred apart in seconds
blending you with Earth and rock
into the roaring puree

To run rapids, you have to trust the river
It isn't an option - you either do or you do
If you resist, the rapids suck you up and
roll you over turning you like a screw
into mortar rocks upside-down
and harder than
forever

If you survive, it will not be because
the river let you go…but
only because you let the river
go

Auto Pilot

Not thinking is hard to do

Heroes will tell you they weren't thinking
when they did heroic things

An act without thinking
is an action of no thought

We are the ones who point this out
by giving admiration as a payment
to ordinary people who do extraordinary things
without thinking

We don't really believe they weren't thinking
except where
we don't
think

Similarities

Women need to love men
Men love to need women
This is a law not a theory of physics
The basic differences between us
become our final similarities

Somewhere beneath us
Where gender is first paralyzed
there is fusion and solidarity
This is why union often feels like reunion
and stuns us into making holidays

Where we are coming from
is always where we are going This is why
Love isn't something you can fall into
by accident

Underneath the skinsoil
We are all rooted at the same author
Not that we are only pawns, mind you
We are also the chessmen, too

Collusion

"You're too crazy for me," he said.
It was an idea that created separation.
To agree to get closer to him
I submitted to his
thought.

I became too crazy for him
and agreed with the idea that
created separation

I arranged all this with him

The laws of exchange

All I ever wanted from anybody
was love

And when I wanted it most
was also when I could have given it most
and didn't

What you want is exactly
what you have to give
this is the law except when
you don't want anything
from anybody which is
liberty

If you want dominion
you have to
conquer yourself,
not
the world

The Thing They Didn't Tell Her

I know a girl who looks good
and feels bad
This is her downfall
because she's afraid it won't last
and she's right!

Looking good is a curse
to the girl who doesn't know
her customer

Beyond what we are creating
is what is creating us
This is always happening right now
It has no beginning and no end
and neither do we... So

Seeing is believing
And NOT seeing is
believing,
too

Being here is not determined by anybody seeing us here and
What we look like is not who we are
This is the thing they didn't
Tell her

Revisions

You kissed me and all the strangers
left my mouth

Where we live

We must be careful
not to confuse the symbols in life
with real living

Legends are grand and so are the icons
But don't confuse REALLY living your life
with a story about someone else's

This is not at all to say that the parables
can't teach us anything This is just to point out
that they can't teach us
everything

We must be vigilant not to become
big fans of gods This is how we can surely
prevent ourselves from becoming gods
ourselves

To be lifted and inspired by someone is everything
but to follow their story would be a grave mistake
The imitation of <u>God</u> is one thing... but
The imitation of gods is something else.

We must be careful to make the distinction
between the symbols of living and real life
There are many of us with discarded wedding rings
in the back of our drawers who could tell you more
For now, just know that ...Your life is not in the story
you tell about yourself
Your life is in the actions you
bring forth
in spite of it

What can only happen now

A miracle happened to us when we let go
and then we got scared

To get it back We reached for the light
covering it by trying too hard we (literally)
got in our own way

We spent 11 years trying valiantly
to HOLD ON to something
that only happens
when I let go

You can never 'get back' to love
It is one of those miracles
that can only happen
now

First Cause

All crimes of the heart
are a result of
arson

Fire is neither good nor bad
we burn in our thinking
first

Human triumph is allied with human despair so perfectly
that pain is often the unlikely instructor of joy
this is how a wild horse can break a man
and how one child with vision can
stop complaining about his mother
and take care of himself

All crimes of the heart begin with separation we must kill
what we love so that we can fully remember
that we are joined to it

Trusting is how we learn to
trust

There is no risk except in your thinking
Whether you lose your mind or it is broken
you will know briefly
what you cannot do
and…you will do it

We look for this in other people
until we find it
in ourselves

Tyranny

Give me absolution
and I turn it into tyranny

I do this because some part
of me is still hoping to control you

I still get God mixed
up with
magic

Here we see it then we don't
who makes this happen...Is it me <u>OR</u> is it you,
or is it me
<u>AND</u> you?

When Too Much Is Not Enough

If you need somebody so much that you think
you will die without them
you probably
will

If you want something so much that you have
to have it you can probably get it but it
won't last

We can't keep what we have to have there
isn't enough of it

Everything that I ever wanted too much
robbed me of what I already had...and
...Our `desperation' for other people
measures as proof how separated
we are from
ourselves

I lost everything I ever lost from fear of
losing it...The FEAR of losing
IS the loss

Every time we push so hard that someone leaves
we can always be sure that it wasn't 'them' we lost,
but ourselves

What's Missing

I'm hiding something and he knows it
Like Him, I won't show my hand
We are both holding something
Back...This is what's missing

At some point in the playing, the game suddenly got serious
The graceful moves went rigid and the easy points went hard
What was sweet went slightly sour...Fear cut the joy in half
There was now a hole in the ball and from this on...At each serve, the
round part went flat and the playing turned
terribly real

He's hiding something and I know it
Like me, he's withdrawing one of his arms
There is some part of him that he doesn't want me to see
...And this is
what's missing

Directions

Belief is only an opinion
It is not enough

It is, often,
too much force

You may lose the star
in passing it

It has taken seconds
to write this down
and years
to pick up the pen

First things First

It isn't necessary
to come true
If we are
True

How we ask

If you think you can hurt somebody
they can probably hurt you because
you think people are
<u>dangerous</u>

If you think you can't hurt somebody
they probably won't hurt you either because
you think people are
<u>harmless</u>

If you can put down the gun
another gun will be put
down

All bullets are multiplied
By two

Frequencies

She cried so loud she became a radio
They did not hear a word she said
...there were so many

Later, she laughed and laughed
but they couldn't figure why
or how they missed it

Trying to understand somebody
is like trying to talk to
somebody

You either do or
you don't

Freedom from Descriptions

The easy part is when we don't know
what we're doing and we do it
anyway

<u>ANYWAY</u> is the catch here…And
the word 'easy'
can be reinvented

The dictionary is a great tool;
but you mustn't allow it to limit you

Use it accordingly
and then
throw it
away

Where Dreams Come from

Dreams don't come to life,
they come FROM life

Paintings Stories Books Babies Statues
These are always here they don't come to us we go to them
They come FROM us so

Daydream all you like
But don't expect anything to magically come TO you
that doesn't come FROM you Because

Even though magic works it doesn't last
You can bring things to you but until
you come to them yourself they are just paintings stories
books babies buildings cities and statues

We don't go TO Paris
until we come FROM Paris I know this sounds crazy
but I promise you it's not a lie.

Vision Vs Seeing

We don't make each other happy we only see each
others happiness

We don't love each other because we're
together We're together because we
love each other

How many times have you ended up
losing the one you wanted most?

As the map is drawn
the road forks
here
...each path will
lead you through
the darkness
yet
...one is longer than the other
and more difficult
to travel

Through a lifetime of choices
we come to know a journey
without distance

How many times have you changed your
mind about dying?

We build the road by walking

The Key

Letting people be whole without us
is how we get to be whole
without them

Where We Come From

The trick is to love with your heart not your head
If you love out of your thinking and not out of your feelings
those we love will feel judged even when
they are cared for

To care for somebody with your head
is just to `believe' you care to care for
someone out of your heart
is to <u>know</u> you do

In our heads, love is just a word we use to name our position on something
we come upon it out of deduction,
we grind it by comparison

In thinking, love is just another noun but
in feeling, it's a verb. It's an <u>action</u> word!
Love isn't in what we `think about doing',
it's <u>what we do</u>.

It's in these actions we take, out of loving
and out of <u>not</u> loving that define who we are

So then Love is not about <u>opinions</u>; it's about <u>choices</u>
It is an act of no comparison and because of this

We don't have to look for the meaning in our lives
it's written down in everything we do

None of what `we think about saying' is heard
no more than what we `thought about doing' gets done
we don't `show up' until we <u>show up So</u>

Who we are and who we <u>think</u> we are
is simply <u>not</u>
the same

When Something Goes Right

I always had a plan for what I'd do
if it didn't work out

I had a few friends I could always count on
mostly because I had repeatedly insisted
that they could count on me This is the sentry
duty of conditional friendships we guard each other
with toy guns and a lot of parliamentary
speech fierce for each other as we could never be
for ourselves and so for pretending this,
we've become it...And besides

I always had a secret plan for what I'd feel
if they didn't come through I'd become a better person
in spite of their betrayal and more than that
I'd get beyond the need for friends
by being my own

You see, I've always had a plan for what I'd do
if it didn't work out I never had (however) a plan
for what I'd do if it DID work out

Receiving love is so much harder than giving it yet
the joke is in offering it, it returns multiplied
leaving me with no plan whatsoever

This is why cats laugh when we make plans.

Precaution

One of the ways I guard
against being alone
is making sure
I will be alone
with somebody

An Optimist Looks At Leaving

I've seen you now at least a hundred times
walk off with your bag over your shoulder briefcase in hand a quick
look back that smile and then you're gone
...Like all migratory birds, you are curious
and reliable

Watching people come and go is how we come
to figure out what <u>doesn't</u>
come and go

People leave but that doesn't always mean
they go away We forget
that the sun going down
is a necessary part of
the sun coming up
again and so,

I bless your 'going away' because I figure
it's just another part of your
'coming back' and means
that we are together
in still another way

What thinking does

If something can't be done
You are thinking of impossibility

If something shouldn't be done
You are thinking of immorality

If something can be done
You are thinking of possibility

If something is done
It is done

The doing of it is just
the doing
of it

Real accomplishment

The accomplishment is not in getting
the home run It's in
hitting the ball

Ask anybody who has a trophy to teach you this
Ask the inventor who has run out of ideas
Ask him if your admiration of his crown
makes him a ruler

If hitting the jackpot is when you are most alive
then your joy is something that can ONLY happen
once in awhile
The trick is to play the game
with your heart wide open because

JOY isn't something that HAPPENS to you
It is something that YOU happen to

Illusions

Owning Real Estate is an illusion

Selling it for profit is good
but it is also an illusion

Ownership and profit
are delicate issues

And this is not something
you have to agree
with

It doesn't matter if it seems right
if it isn't
true

What musicians taught me

I am an interpreter
All writing is just interpretation of what is so
I don't kid myself about
being a (so called) author I know that

Even when I make things out of air,
I have an accomplice
I am not the source of music
I just play it…And let's face it

Knowing that life can go on without us
is enough to make anybody
creative

What women must forgive

My mother died of an enlarged heart
this is the physical metaphor
and there is a theological irony
attached

The muscle grows were we pump it hard
This is strength
not power

Not seeing you is vision, too
This is how I've come to bring flowers
to friends who are not
in the hospital

If a woman can't forgive a man his life
Then she must carry him in her chest until
it breaks

The Shift

What we might consider is
how we are good
rather than
how
good we are

Duet For One

A mirror is one way to
look at yourself

What we see is
what we think
and looking at it is why
we have mirrors

Image is exact only in image
A case in point is the original
against the xerox

A copy is a way of keeping things alive
Imitation is about permanence

Being constant is impossible
as we know being
constant

Being here is exact only
in being here So

Mirrors shatter
and we are doubled up
a thousand
ways

How you can be a church

So confused were they by the original
that they only sang on
Sunday

The mystery here is that there is
no mystery And

Things mean what you want them
to mean

We can suffer this or not there is only
to choose to live your life from the majority laws or
from yourself The heart, being uniquely yours,
will follow or lead

The secret is there is
no secret…And

You can sing anytime you want

What we can't have

Let them have their funny clothes
so we can have our funny
clothes

Let them have their songs
so we can have our songs because
it isn't about songs, it's about
music

It's what we resist
that we can't have

The Trick

The mistake is
to make bad out of
good

The way to fix it is
to make good out of
bad

The trick is not to tell the story
like it's about somebody else.

How we become whole

Embarrassment
is a good lesson in
humility

We can turn a mistake
into something
else

We are learning to be whole
by breaking into
pieces

Why we steal

Until we know that there is enough
for everybody
we steal

It is always today

Failure is not about
getting there

Success is
not about NOT
getting
there

There is NO
there
here

The wonder of words

Better I not say anything
than to speak so easily about hard things

Better I say nothing
and you not listen
except to hear too much

This is the wonder of words
and their embarrassment

Time

Time cannot run out

The Eleven Communications

Make me hard

Make me come

Give me money

Is it mine?

Where is it?

How much will it cost?

Will it last?

Is it true?

What does it mean?

and

Can I keep it

The Eleven Observations

Dogs know stuff

Timing is everything but it can't be timed

Everyone I didn't like secretly reminded me of myself

Not everybody stops at the stop sign

If you want to be happy, nobody can stop you

Some people live and learn; some people just live

Friends are the people who recognize us

She didn't know it couldn't be done so she went ahead and did it

A promise is only a wish

What loves does not wear out

And

A stitch in time really does save nine

The Eleven Revelations

Love is a verb

Life is now all at once

All songs come from the same music

Many are called; but few are called back

The "HAVE NOTS" have it, too

Simple does not mean easy

Rich people are just poor people with money

Love does not stopt

Where we come from really is where
we are going

Cigarettes really can cause cancer'
And
Cancer really can cause healing

What we Pray About

We don't know what we'll do if it happens
we pray about this

And if we don't trust
by answers we trust by questions

One night the dam bursts the tidal wave is released
from the place where we kept it
All the wrinkles appear from where they were hidden
all the years of smoking come due at once
and there's no more to see but
seeing

We fully live an idea and we fully die it
then there is only
life…Life is what we are looking for

We don't know how we feel about this
It is what we pray about

Then we give up seeing…After that we either smile
all the time of get another idea
This is the reunion
they talk about in books
about the love of other people

Loving other people is what we're looking for
as other people…It is what we pray about

Reversing Nature

Hey wait a minute
we don't stop loving people
end the whole idea and start up with another partner
This is not mating

You can't really end a true partnership
this is what I've been confused about
I have asked to be whole not divided into shares

We don't stop loving one person when we start loving another person
love doesn't stop
you can't stick it in by the flower

<u>That is how we reverse nature</u> we have no right to do this
and arrogant fools that we are neither have we a way

We can't end the source on either end
we were made to be in the center
this is why December brings us home and why
April draws us out
the circle still surprises us because we think we have an edge
we still think we can 'get ahead' of the others but
I promise you we are not different than the birds in the trees
except that we leave our young and
break our promises

Don't tell me that other people have nothing to do with this and
I won't pretend that you are dragging death on your index finger

I don't know about you but I didn't start here

Perfection

The thing is not
to HAVE a good time but
to BE a good time.

Perfection is a choice
You can choose it
or not...it is no matter
In the scheme of things,
it is choosing you

We can't be different without being similar first

It's great to jump out of the 'story'
exhilarating to draw the map instead of just following it
Yet we must beware not to lose our minds while
we're out of them

And when we're out there beyond what we know
We must keep a string tied to the gate
And not refer to those we leave behind us as 'them'

If we forget that 'they' are also 'us'
We could lose ourselves,
and each other

We mustn't confuse being 'unlimited' with being
'out of control'
There is a subtle difference between these twins
As us, they are alike yet not the same
We cannot let the boundaries blur,
even when there are none

continued

Don't get me wrong, I still want to go to the moon
I haven't been there in years
...The only caution that I have
is that we make sure to travel as individuals,
and that we start out whole
before we join

This is the trick of tricks
To know first and then
to dare

Signs of Life

The sign on the highway
says 'YIELD'

Oh the genius of the symbol
to be so symbolic

How often have I taken a 'stand' on something
and missed the point?

Legislative action
is the way man agrees or disagrees
with nature

And nature is proof we are
not final Although we
end...And

Yield is the word we use
to point forward and join
motion

It's a sign on the highway

Semantics

If I tell you I can't love more than one
person at a time
I'm not talking about love
I'm talking about
control

What you taught me'

I want to thank you for allowing me to touch you
It is how I came to touch myself
again

One move of unity and I knew
that being free has nothing at all to do
with getting out

This is not just another way of holding on
although it is about how
we are connected

Attached to this there are no opticals
There are no photographs here about the strangers
who stole your Mother
Nobody will pick you up and drop you
on your head

This is what the master tried to teach us
This is what we couldn't understand
except to know it

I want to thank you for asking me
for everything
...Until you did I never dreamed
I had it

Irony

What we're looking for
is looking for us too

The Distinction

Love isn't something that looks
for the best in someone
...Love finds it

Non-Resistance

If you can't resist something
you'll probably get some
part of it

If you accept it
you can have the whole
thing

Lessons in being easy

To be is to be something
Not to be is to be nothing

To be nothing
is a requirement
of no thing

To be something
is a requirement
of some thing

To be some body is the same
as being some thing

To be nobody related to everybody is the
hardest part of being easy

Intention

To pretend
is to dream
awake

How we look for love

A person can tell you the truth
without ever knowing that they've said true
things

Someone you hardly know can be the one who teaches you about your
Father

Think of the brief smiles exchanged in
elevators the friendly hands that have
carried your grocery bags there are
many missionaries who are not named

We look for love
as though it's
not here

Cartography

At some point without realizing it
I crossed a line
from which I cannot return
and yet
I know I shall come to it again

What is ahead is
also behind
yet
We can't get there by going
back

Information about Kings

He was a good stage actor
but he did not feel comfortable
on film

Something in him was uneasy with the
vanity of the camera

...We must be fools
to be kings

This is a hard thing to know
about kings

What writers forget

I thought I had to write in order to live
...I had forgotten
that I had to live
in order to
write

My life doesn't come out of my writing
my writing
comes out of my life

Advice for Young Writers from an Old Poet

Don't write like a great writer
…just write

From from yourself
not to yourself

…And mostly

Never tell a story
like it isn't
about you

When remembering doesn't work

Don't start remembering
the men you could have
married

If you used to be alive
What are you now?
vinegar against oil?
water looking for a
fire?

Trust the seed. Annie
There is a genius
in going
on

Remembering how it <u>was</u> is one of the ways
we avoid how it <u>is</u>

Being there is how we avoid
being
<u>here</u>

Providence

There is a third part to every two people who join
some call it 'spirit'

Truth is not told any clearer than
the experience
of this

Another word for luck is
providence

We are Co-Creators
This is how art
imitates
God

The Cost of Not Living

I always thought I had a lot to say
until I couldn't say it
...Only when I couldn't talk
did I realize how much
I <u>didn't</u> have
to say

Just about when we think we have life figured out
it comes up with another custard pie
...We learn <u>value</u> by <u>going</u>
<u>broke</u>

When I knew <u>everything</u>,
I didn't need much education
...We don't know what we don't have
until it <u>shows up</u> as
missing

We think we have it covered
until we can't cover it
Life is fair until it doesn't work
...It isn't until our name falls off,
that we even begin to know
who we are

going blind is one of the best things
that ever happened to me
...It was only when I lost sight of everything
that I realized how little I could see

continued

Getting lost is one of the surest ways
we challenge ourselves to find
a way back but to stop is another thing

Not moving forward is the cost
Of not living

Don't mine for gold in a Jewelry Store

Don't think so much
you'll wear out
the miracle

There is still some root of magic in you
that won't accept the wizard
as a man

It's hard to play Hamlet when you know
the joke....This is what burns you

Don't mine for gold in a jewelry store

The Cost of Giving

We can get what we give
This is the
instruction

What we can accept, we can give away
and have it, too

The cost of true GIVING
is to receive

The difference between Men and Women

Men want to go to bed
with women
And
Women want to wake up
with men

Lovers are born too
Except that women are
Girls first
And
Men become boys

It happens early on
…Little girls will always touch you
If you love them
And Little boys will always love you
If you touch them

This is the difference
Between men and women

Common Sense

If you want peace;
Don't yell about it

Your Business

Don't let me terrorize
you because I am a
thinker

It's only the
spirit that can touch
you anyway not me

If you look closer, you will see
that these are
just words and all I do
is write them down

What you think about them
is your own
business

Holding Patterns

...Peace as <u>survival</u> is <u>not</u> peace at all

The First Fuel

Standing still
is how we learn to value actions that don't
move...yet something is moved

This is the great illusion
...that we find salvation first
in each other for awhile?

we learn a lot from magicians
Mystery is the first fuel
And the last

The Trinity Duet

Every church has an entrance
and an exit...this is how we learn
to limit our devotion

Belonging to one church
apart from another church
is how we learn separation

Each religion has its holy men
and its heretics

This how we come to make
priests different from ourselves

All hearts have two bells
the first one rings and we ask
the second rings and it answers
As a result of the first two
a THIRD thing happens

Each religion has it's holy bells
the first one rings and we ask
the second rings and it's an answer
This duet creates the trinity

And...It's the third part
that makes the first two
show up

What Sees

Beyond the view of things,
the muse is out there making custard pies
...Nature is `reliable'
far beyond our knowing

Life goes on and on
in ways we've not imagined

We learn to trust when there is hardly
anything to count on

Way beyond what we see
is not just what `sees' us
..it's the `seeing'
itself

Providence

When we recognized each other
we are familiar

When two of us
reach out to one loving
we are the idea of spirit

Truth is not told
any clearer than this

This experience of spirit
is the third partner
of two who join

Another word for this is
Providence

Providence is
the language
of discovering what already is

Providence is spirit
showing up

What Becomes Clear

No man can fill the girl
who has lost her father
and every man can fill the woman
who never had one

SEPaRATION

Separation is something from the
old books

I don't know about it anymore
It is something I have forgotten

I see the alteration in the lens but not in the
source

Things can be interpreted again
That's what we're doing
now

Separation is an old idea
and didn't
last

I can't even comprehending it
now

Except as the other side of this

Peripheral Vision

He doesn't have to say this out loud
The conversation around him doesn't
INCLUDE him including me
...What more names me that this not naming?

Oh the volume of the things we do not say

The Irony of Self Promotion

Everything he ever accused me of
Was about him

We are always secretly leaving those people
We cannot trust
…Not because they are untrustworthy
but because
WE are untrustworthy

Where Dreams Come From

Dreams don't come to life,
they come FROM life

Paintings Stories Books Babies Statues
These are always here
they don't come to us we go to them
They come FROM us so

Daydream all you like
But don't expect anything to magically come TO you
that doesn't come FROM you Because

Even though magic works
it doesn't last

We don't go TO Paris
until we come FROM Paris I know this sounds crazy
but I promise you it's not a lie.

Sharing 101

SHARING is not dividing up property
it is not giving something away.

SHARING is GIVING our part FREELY

Joy isn't what we're doing
JOY is how we FEEL about what
we're doing

and SHARING is not when you give up part
of something because you have to

SHARING is how we can teach people
what is already theirs

Nothing true is diminished by sharing it

What Happens Anyway

Maturity is following nature
into submission

Wisdom is following submission
into nature

And thinking about it
doesn't do any
good

Getting Off The High Horse

The man I love is somebody's Father
it is a romantic idea
It relates me to the women
in legends

There is someplace I can go from here and not die
I have stretched my senses to this and
I want to love you like your Mother
did

We are two people trying to get back to where
we already are

Children are made from people
it is how we ask

I only lose you
when I'm lost

How We Recognize Each Other

Feeling our own pain is how we got into this in the
first place

Causing pain is how we measured the
half

And then we admitted they were the same
holding onto a difference

Other people's pain is what teaches us
about how much pain we are in

Suffering is the teacher
Love is how we recognize
each other

Caring about it is religious

Without nature, there is no student
…Birds can't teach us everything

This is a trick of course,
All lovers were magicians first

Falling in love is a good metaphor
Without romance it would be too easy

Simple is how we insult it
the other way

I always loved you today

The LAW

We say there is no God
and then we get everything we asked for
including no God
...This is how perfect
the law works

And because we are a little wise
We call intervention luck and
worse than that
...we're not surprised

Julian Simon knows this and so does
Charlie Brown who said "Lucy, I only know
that what goes up must
come down"

And so we dream of a better life
preparing for the worst and this is how
we miss the
joke

We are so inept in our attempts to protect
ourselves from death
that we also protect ourselves
from life

We say there is no God
We say there are no miracles, too
but only when they're
missing

The Most Valuable Men

The one who encourages you
to actually be who you are
is to be knighted
...Not only because he is perfect,
anybody can be perfect, but because
he allows perfection
in others

The men who <u>know</u> you are valuable are
the most valuable men

We can only take people where
they are actually willing
to be
We don't love each other because we're
together
We're together because we
love each other

Where We Come From

The trick is to love with our heart, not our head
If you love out of our thinking and not out of our feelings
those we love will feel judged even when
they are cared for

To care for somebody with our head
is just to `believe' you care to care for
someone out of our heart
is to <u>know</u> you do

In our heads, love is just a word we use to name our position on something
we come upon it out of deduction,
we grind it by comparison

In thinking, love is just another noun but
in feeling, it's a verb. It's an <u>action</u> word!
Love isn't in what we `think about doing',
it's <u>what we do</u>.

It's in these actions we take, out of loving
and out of <u>not</u> loving that define who we are

So then, Love is not about <u>opinions</u>;
it's about <u>choices;</u> It is an act of no comparison
and because of this

We don't have to look for the meaning in our lives
it's written down in everything we do

continued

None of what `we think about saying' is heard
no more than what we `thought about doing' gets done
we don't `show up' until we show up So

Who we are and who we think we are
is simply <u>not</u> the same

Relearning Perception

Anybody who's any good as telling stories
never tells you everything he knows
...The truth, written down, just doesn't work
What we see starts with us, that's why it keeps returning
...We can get as big as any game we play
but none of us get
bigger

The Examined Life

Through a lifetime of choices
we come to know a journey
without distance

We build the road by
walking

Reliability

I always thought that love would get me through
Even when the wind is above my wings
Something in me reaches

I've never been afraid to be afraid
It was feeling nothing that scared me…So

Giving in is easy for me
…Giving up, however
is another thing

I believe that some part of us is so true
That even when we die…something in us
Lives…So

I counted on goodwill and lived by my intention
I took my little life and put it on the fire
I never dreamed that providence would not prevail
…but now and then love is really not enough and
sometimes Goliath beats the crap out of David

This is what taught me the value of the 'rewrite'

Early Propaganda

Who told you to marry your own
and what was the
difference?

What is this business about your being one way
and my being another?

Where is the separation?

Who told you who you should cherish
who you should push away?

And don't think I won't point out
that your excuses wear out

...How can I hide where I
am the same?

Who was lying to you when you were listening?

Who wasn't listening to you
when you told the truth?

ARRIVALS and DEPARTURES

Men come; women yearn

Turning Point

One day you just stop looking
for the right person
and just become
the right person

You Can Dream

I am born to bear this
You are surprised by my not knowing
the trends

You see me
that is just the beginning

It is not only me - it is also you
<u>and</u> me We are an edition
of this We are made to be seen
To come
and go

"You can dream about this"
that's all I ever had to
say about anything

"You can dream!"

You can unlock your father's failure with one hug
"You can dream"
You can turn fear
into a circus
with one move

Here & There

Remembering is the opposite
of being HERE now
it is being THERE
now

Intervention

You are my intervention, Peter
it matters not at all if we have
fresh flowers or a house
Your INTENTION
is a home to me

I have met you now
we are on the other side
of everyone This is why I am willing
to bless every hand that holds you
because I know now that it is actually (in some way)
my own And So

I celebrate everyone who touches you, including me

Before I knew you before I knew myself
I was in the hands you held
I am in the bed
you shared with someone else
...I am the one who opened the blinds

I see you at every age and every boy who smiles
at me is you
I know what feeds you, Peter
I know what grows

You can't teach me this I know it by heart
I know that being used is being lifted to some purpose
I know what moves us I know what lives and
I know what cannot die

continued

Even at your leaving
you will come
across the circle
like all of nature and the sun before us

I will not bear your resignation
I will howl and you will hear me
Even in the grave

What Isn't Missing

I want to know what it is in you
that responds to me

I want to know why I don't give up
when I give in

I want to know what part of you
knows the part of me that
lies

I want to see what's missing

I want to know what third part
makes us one

I want to look at you terror
and see if it is mine

I want to love you where
I want to be
loved

I want to see what isn't missing

Crossing the Line

Peter, I'm counting on you to stay alive
You can do this for me I know you can
this is why I chose you
to take the wheel

Peter, I will go with you around the circles/you know I will
That's why I cried when you wouldn't stop
I wanted to mark the lines
also, I wanted you
to cross it

I've learned this much about flying In order
to defy the laws of gravity
You must follow them first
and don't hate me
for saying this
you can love me, too

Looking out for you is one of the ways I look out for myself
I know that "it's not safe" that's why you're
counting on me to stay alive
that's why you marked the line
So I would cross it

Lee, I will go around the circles you know I would
This is why I tried to stop you and
This is why I couldn't

HomeMaking

Being married to Paul was like dancing with Fred Astaire
Life was easy and opulent and elegant
Everything I did was perfect to him
…Everything I said was brilliant and had value
He was devoted, deeply compassionate and true
I was loved and lifted, cared for and celebrated
And I left him for a coward who couldn't dance
…At certain angles, in certain light
He looked exactly like my father
His name was Lee
Like yours

When I met you I couldn't believe the irony
Yet you were so unlike the other Lee
…so brave and loving and

Being loved by Jim Miller was like being loved by God
It was pure, unconditional, clean and uncomplicated
The house was filled with jasmine and fresh fruit
Bach played the soundtrack to our lives
Great friends, gourmet food
He gave me stature, status and an English garden
And I left him for a two-bit actor who had no soul
…At certain times, when I least expected
He would forget himself and touch me in a sacred way
His name was Lee
Like yours

continued

Since I know you I have tried not to call you by your name
I could never fit it in my mouth for you
My heart did not match the name
And yet I love you more than any one of them

Peter had a plane and a house in Capri
He took me to Paris for breakfast after our first dinner
He bought me a friendly country house on a hill
...He didn't mind when I wrote all night
He built me a library and a grand piano
He was charmed by talent and tried to steal it
So I left him for TV director who didn't want my talent
Who would love me and leave me at the drop of a hat
His name was Lee
Like yours

Lee resented me because he wanted me
But he always left me for a far more sinister reason
...He left me because he loved me...I knew this
And didn't change my number until
The day he died

I tell you this now because I know you are leaving me
I want you to know that I will never leave you
It's not because you're name is Lee
It's because I know you don't want to

I believe that we are a combination of these mistakes
And you can't tell me I'm not all the women you ever left
I know we have a destiny to make it right
The only thing we'll lose if we don't try
Is everything

continued

Don't you dare tell me at this crossroad that you don't know who I am
and I won't lie and say that it's okay for you to go
We're not finished, Lee
…Not yet

We not finished until we learn to dance like Fred Astaire
Until we have a garden and a grand piano
We're not finished until we stop bellyaching
Admit we're in this together and
Make a home

What I Haven't learned

I haven't learned anything since I was Eleven.
That's when I stopped learning.
My education continued for many years after that
But all I got was information

Even after I had loved and lost
I loved again
…Every time I was hit with a custard pie
I always thought it was funny

I earned and lost a fortune
Was given grace from God
And still slept in
Nobody had more than me for awhile
And then nobody had less

I should have learned something from this
But all I got was information

When I was Eleven I learned that God is Love
And it turned out to be absolutely true
God is Love…but don't fool yourself
…You also have to get it in writing.
We will no longer live in the same world

This is the book I hoped I'd never write
The book where I'm forced to spit your name out of my mouth

What Won't happen

We'll never go to the Miyako in San Francisco
You'll never meet Jack
You won't know Ben when he is finally
the majestic beast we hoped he's be

I won't know if you are sick or in a crash
No one will tell me if you're hurt
I will no longer know your number by heart
In time, I won't even recognize
Your car

The day you die no one will tell me
No one will call or bring soup
Although we may live many years under the same sky
We close here on a writers page
This is the book where you leave my life
And enter my work
It takes no talent to write when your heart is broken

Laura will get married in September
And PJ and Lisa will follow
Someday little girls dressed like ice cream cones
Will sing you Happy Birthday at the table where I write these very words

Everything I might have felt for you or yours
Is now rewritten ……You will not know or even bow your head
When Emily finally goes home and I bury her in a little yellow box
Out in my yard

It's so easy to forget
What we couldn't possibly even remember
continued

This is the book where we reverse the tiller
Where our home together becomes just another house
This is the book where I must forget that I will love you forever
…The book I said I'd never write

A Promise

It's astonishing to me how casually
people who loved deeply
simply discard each other
never to know or see that person again
As if they knew or loved each other at all
It is as if they died
actually cut out of memory…Slap, it's over

I need you to know something…I will not let you die
I will not forget that you are beloved to me
…It will be extremely sad to live without you
Not knowing you is impossible to me

I don't understand it
People who were profoundly connected
Become virtual strangers again
Forfeiting children yet fighting for property
They dismiss partnership
As though it was simply a mistake

People break apart their lives as though
Relationships don't have value
Is love so easy to find
That we can casually stop it
Must we live to remember love
In all its absences

The Power of our thinking

He was afraid they wouldn't make it
she picked up on this and
It became as real to her
As anything she herself believed

This is the power of prejudice
It is a blindness so profound
That we can only see what
We actually want to see

And it works backwards too
…Fear revises memory
Paul called this 'selective remembering'
It's why he had to wake me up

We miss whole lifetimes
Afraid of being truly alive

Measurements

We measure our lives
by what we can afford to buy
rather than what we
can't afford to lose

And finally there was you

I knew your eyes by heart at the first reading
I could repeat them in detail...oh and when I met you
I felt 'known', as though I had been recognized
...as though I had been actually seen
and not just looked at

Blindfolded, I could kiss a thousand lips
And know your lips..oh god and when you
entered me you entered and entered
You made my heart come
Hair tousled, blessed and sexy
And Ahhhhhhhh...so very, very happy.

It was the closest I've ever been
To another human being...closer than
The babies once inside me
You were ALL me and
I was ALL you
Your senses rhyme with my senses
Our bodies locked and rocking
Rocking...You made me HOME

You give meaning and light to everything
I feel so lucky to love you
To be loved ...no more pagan amnesia when I twist
my legs into a towel..no more falling exhausted like a bad penny
into my feathered bed

continued

You have untied all my mistakes
There is no tear in the fabric where you stop
You fill me so fully that all other lovers leave my mouth
It was always you
…even then

I'm so happy you're finally here

Final Observations

Real vision is not contaminated
by thought nor is it reducible to
language except as an
action

Wisdom and learning are quite different
Learning is always of things
External...Wisdom is higher sanity
It is knowing

PEACE is NOT the opposite
of anything although
IT includes
everything including the language
which gets in
its way

To explain it would be to contain IT
IT is not containable

IT shows up in art and all the languages
Not when we try to measure it or define it I
IT shows up when the actions we take
are FELT

I say SHOW UP
yet IT is always here

continued

To live a FELT life
to BE REALLY ALIVE
is not about following your thinking
(the language limits you to logic)
...It is about following
your heart

About the Author

Merrit Malloy is a best selling author, award winning screenwriter and poet. She is the author of 28 books and enjoys a worldwide following. She lives in Santa Barbara, California and has two beautiful, spirited daughters and one spectacular grandson, Jack Riley.

Printed in Great Britain
by Amazon

77639524R00089